I0532438

Cities On a Hill

Josh Urban

ISBN: 979-8-9864197-1-8 (paperback edition.)
ISBN: 979-8-9864197-2-5 (e book edition.)

www.JoshUrban.com

1 A Press
Box 783
Rustburg, VA 24588

Acknowledgments

*Special thanks to: the activities team at
Statler Place, the floor staff, Hill City Writers, Terri St. Cloud,
Bob Finson, Jen Bee, Noah Urban,
Bob Urban, Leah Weiss, Dave Metzger, and
the residents & their families.*

*Cover design by Noah Urban
www.Mazuzu.com*

This work is dedicated to Martha, and all the others who
suffered and shone with such grace.

You've forever changed me.

Chapter 1 - *The Sparrow*

"Josh."

I looked around the lunchroom of the ordinary retirement home on Callahan Avenue. The sunbeams, still unregulated, peeped in the windows. The mood inside was glum, obedient, compliant.

One resident per table, each table six feet apart, all residents facing the same way.

My mask itched, things kept going wrong —and I was dangerously close to turning into my shirt.

Business casual acted like a bad friend.

I naively hoped for respectability, but influence corrupted. It dragged me down to the insincerity of rumpled polyester.

Did they discover the phrase "it's not my department" in the wrinkles of a no-iron shirt, like a crumb of a hastily eaten sandwich?

The stress was constant, the COVID lockdown indefinite. The position of house entertainer had turned into activities director. Things were complicated.

Quasi-martial law pushed a thousand daily reasons for moral compromise. Vision, inner and outer, often blurred. It seemed easy to become as faded, jaded, and plastic as my cheap clothes.

The tremulous voice piped up again, somewhere near my elbow.

"Josh, can I talk to you?"

I looked down into the face of a memory.

When I was a boy, I helped an injured bird, holding it gently and praying. It was all I could do. Its tiny feathers spoke of a fierce dignity, with wings that knew more of wind and sky than I ever would.

Martha looked up at me like that sparrow.

She grasped my hand with a surprising strength. Her hair was archetypal grandma white and curly, her frame small and bent. She was mostly deaf, and spoke with a shaky voice, but knew absolutely her opinion about most anything.

I knelt by the lonely table. Resisting the urge to turn plastic, I concentrated and returned Martha's gaze through her thick glasses.

"Josh, I had a dream."

"Oh?"

"I had a dream that we wrote a book together about our time here....And you made a million dollars!"

"Hey, I *like* that!"

She continued. "Yes, and the publisher called me to arrange a second printing."

"*Nice!* Can I tell the room?"

"No, no, it'll be our little secret for now. Don't forget about us, Josh, okay?"

Her voice cut through the blur of stress. Her glasses became mirrors, reflecting my face, and the choice between up and down that waited around every corner in the building.

"I won't. And, if I ever write a book, I'll dedicate it to you."

I squeezed the Sparrow's hand, rose, and went back to the land of polyester.

She went to bingo.

The sunbeams shone on Callahan Avenue many times since then, slowly bleaching the carpet and gnawing the patio chairs, the teeth of Time.

I moved away, and swapped polyester for flannel. Spring came stealing over the mountain, and blazed into another summer.

If I listen closely, beyond the Blue Jay in the pecan tree and crickets in the pasture, there's something else.

Somewhere between the rocking chair and my conscience —there it is again. A question intones in a quavery voice as I sit at my keyboard. Maybe it's her ghost. Or maybe it's just what's right.

"Josh, will you tell them?"

"Yes I will, Martha."

This one's for you.

Author's Note

Between March 2020 and December 2021, I worked directly with elderly residents of "Statler Place" during the COVID-19 lockdown. Identifying information has been changed. This could have, and did, happen anywhere. Their days, suffering, and grace remained hidden to all but a few.

This is a witnessing.

COVID-19 Community Timeline

2020 *(Listed names are residents)*

Jan 11 - First COVID death reported in Wuhan, China.

Jan 20 - First US case reported.

Jan 23 - Wuhan locks down.

Jan 31 - HHS declares public health emergency.

March 11 - WHO declares COVID a pandemic.

March 13 -16 - State of national emergency.
States start to lock down, "15 Days to slow the spread" announced.

March 17 - Doors lock at Statler Place, no family for St. Patrick's Day.

April 3 - CDC issues mask guidance.

April 12 - No family for Easter.

May 8 - Unemployment hits 14.7%.

May 18 - Bernice dies (not of COVID).

May 20 - States start to unlock, nursing homes still locked.

July 4 - No family for Independence Day.

July 21 - Outdoor visits start at Statler Place (canceled in case of 14 day quarantines). Indoor visits still prohibited.

Aug 25 - New testing requirements for nursing homes.

Oct 24 - Coach dies (not of COVID).

Oct 31 - No family for Halloween.

Nov 12 - Ms. Harriet dies (not of COVID).

Nov 26 - No family for Thanksgiving.

Dec 25 - No family for Christmas.

Dec 31 - No family for New Year's Eve.

2021

Jan 12 - Miss Golden dies (not of COVID).

Feb 18- Vaccine available to residents.

March 1 - Trailer visits (a portable room in the parking lot) scheduled at Statler Place.

March 3 - Outbreak puts trailer visits on hold (14 days).

March 17 - Indoor visits resume at Statler Place, with appointment, a year after original closure.

March 19 - Vaccinated staffer tests positive, doors lock for 14 days. Indoor visits prohibited. Two more identical new cases reset lockdown.

April 14 - Indoor visits resume.

April 28 - 2nd floor tests positive, quarantines for 14 days. Other floors unaffected.

May 15 - Governor opens restaurants to full capacity, relaxes other restrictions. Nursing homes unchanged.

July 16 - Ms. Val dies (not of COVID).

July 29 - Positive locks down building. Delta variant likely.

Aug 5 - Leon Wilbur dies (not of COVID).

Sept 2 - All visits canceled.

Sept 6 - No family for Labor Day.

Sept 12 - Some wings allowed outdoor visits.

Sept 21 - Indoor Visits resume.

Oct 17 - Positive, 1st floor locks, outbreak rules change.

Oct 21 - Visits resume. Weekly testing remains for staff.

December 24 - Sam dies (possibly of COVID).

Dec 28 - Josh's last day of work at Statler Place.

Postscript: 2023

March 13 - Mask mandates end at Statler Place.

April 10 - State of national emergency terminated, originally declared March 13, 2020. Voluntary masking still common in stores and other public places.

May 1 - *Cities on a Hill* released. Public health emergency declared Jan. 31, 2020 slated to expire May 11, 2023.

Chapter 2 - *The Hula Dancer*

Late March, 2020: If there had been a tiny hula dancer on the dashboard, she would have stood frozen. The faded asphalt, eerie, empty, without a car, reflects a sinister gray back to the vacant sky.

My little red Kia fits the plastic of the town. But today, something is wrong. I never had a front row seat at the light before. Where are the shoppers, choking the road with their financed-shiny cars? The idle youths mingling with seagulls in the mall parking lot, stealing pretzels and shoes?

An unnatural hush snarls over this Jerusalem of the middle class. Even Jesus of Suburbia stays home, stays safe.

The laminated card in the glove box validates me. "Josh Urban is an essential employee of Statler Place, permitted to travel." I'd always hoped for a special pass, an all-access tour card. But not like this.

The accolades cost eight thousand points on the DOW and a national shattering. Some say Fear smells like iron. I think it's more like the alcohol bite of hand sanitizer.

If there had been a tiny hula dancer on the dashboard, she might have worn a miniature mask, and tried to smile with her eyes. She would have failed.

Once upon a time when fist-bumps were still a sign of strength and friends could disagree, I had been an electric guitarist. That slid into DJing—primarily for the old folks. "Hey all you OG's! Here's a club banger from '56!"

I had worked the nursing home circuit in the metropolitan area, dancing with ladies who remembered James Brown on the radio, and befriending men who had worked for a living.

The new Kia—not *quite* a Ferrari—is the fruit of my creative entrepreneurship. My modest house shelters a floor-to-ceiling record collection.

There are 13 guitars, a wood shop, no pets, blinds, but no frilly curtains and no TV (by choice). While a good life for a twenty-something, at 34, it's not the only thing starting to gray.

My situation crept onto a beloved graphic tee with a silhouette of Peter Pan. Words on the chest loudly proclaim "I'M SO FLY I NEVERLAND."

Any potential Mrs. Urban begged to differ. *And all I got was a lousy T shirt.* An ex-girlfriend had chided me about my choice of hats. I just laughed, but an awful lot of life does seem to roll off the flat neon brim. Am I hiding from something? Maybe the lid is sheltering me from an instructing rain. And why do I delight in "getting away" with things, from colorful styles to loud guitars?

After a day of stickin' it to the Man, I sit and listen to jazz records in my hipster-approved creative professional living room. But they always end, leaving silence, the antique clock tick-tick-ticking away in the empty darkness. How loud the echoes are.

Jordan Peterson's *12 Rules For Life* finds its way to the stack of books under my vintage lamp. It will prove transformative. Is a happy life as a perennial youth a possible, or even worthy, aim?

Is happiness itself something to be pursued?

(What about Meaning?)

Maturity lurks around the corner— with a sledgehammer.

An Honorary Grandson in Happier Times

Back when smiles were legal, I'd host a monthly party for the residents at Statler Place. It turned into programming a few times a week.

We formed *The Thinkers Club*, discussing plants, fossils, arrowheads, trains, and history — the world's, and theirs.

January 1st, 2020 dawned a gentle Wednesday—club day, uneventful.

"Welcome to the roaring twenties! What resolutions should we make? Whatcha say, Sam? How 'bout an adventure?"

One was on the way, unseen, unavoidable. Like any adventure, it would profoundly change the participants. Some would even die.

It Begins

Waves of static wake me each morning, the clock radio a growing foghorn of news.

The Fear in the East draws closer, and things start to shift. As the waves crash on the shore, the executive director stops me in the hall one morning after a *Thinker's Club.*

"What's your DJ event calendar look like?" Steve asks, with eyes of a Marine ready to kick doors.

"It's empty" I reply. The panic is setting in.

My regular customers keep calling. "Just a few weeks, Josh, till this whole thing blows over. Stay safe out there."

Stay safe? How can I afford to eat?

Steve has a job offer, a life raft.

"Can you be here five days a week, and entertain the troops? Music in the hall, reading, magic tricks, anything?"

Scuttling off to a corner by the pool table, I frantically punch numbers on the calculator app.

Okay, okay. My phone trembles in my hand.

Can I live? Yes.

"Done!"

"Done!"

The doors lock on St. Patrick's day.
It's hard to be festive at the half-party we have planned for the residents, but we try. The staffers dance hysterically, I spin Bing Crosby records. Forget Irish eyes - none are smiling. But we try.

We've got to be brave.

The waves turn into a tsunami. One day half the nurses are wearing masks. Soon, they're mandatory. Goggles won't be far away. The seas rise along with the adrenaline levels. The media gleefully throws us anchors, and we start to sink. Somewhere through the madness, I will become the Activities Director.

On Not Throwing Plates

The CDC, the governor, the State Department of Health, and the management of Statler Place set rules—lots of them, to a crushing effect. The residents are restricted (often to their rooms), and families are forbidden— except for deathbed visits (with masks, goggles, gloves, and gowns). The lockdowns will last a year before a hint of thawing, and then gradually cede with wrenching starts and stops.

At the time of this writing in early 2023, when I returned for a visit, I was requested to wear a mask.

Nobody is held forcibly, but where can they go? Some are content, many are miserable, others go insane.

All are inspirational in some way.

But to whom? Their families can get as far as the tinted windows and Zoom calls. Friends might as well be in Siberia. Only essential staff are permitted. Step by step, the isolation becomes inhuman.

How easily we yield.

The Old endure, patiently, stoically. The skeleton crew trudges through the halls, witnessing.

We sail on together, and the ship creaks as it tosses into the Unknown.

The "In it Together" government ads taunt with an Orwellian laugh and hip letters: *Just two more weeks.*

It also doesn't work.

COVID comes creeping anyway. (Years later, the debates will start: *Should the doors have been locked?*)

Rigorous "PCR testing" is mandated by the state. Each resident is tested weekly, and staff twice-weekly. If a resident on a floor tests positive, that floor locks. If a staffer travels between floors and tests positive, all floors lock. The tests take places on an enormous scale.

The test technology has a small but not insignificant error rate, and now, controversies about efficacy. By late 2021, out of 20 positive returns (resulting in lockdowns), 19 are "asymptomatic" at Statler Place.

Strangely, nobody throws plates.

Good actions have a way of blazing through the darkest of nights. A city set on a hill *cannot* be hid, even if sentenced to solitary confinement "for its own good."

Good Morning

The little red Kia wheels up to the same spot each day. The old ladies like to know who's there, so I take to parking where they can see.

"Thanks Mom, have a good day."

I hang up the phone, and sit for a moment.

Okay, I'm here.

What can be done to help, to slow the slide into madness, to get all of us through? The question waits in the parking lot of Statler Place every day, ready to knock my teeth out. I see it in the eyes of the geese wandering menacingly across the broken asphalt.

Peterson's *12 Rules For Life* ideas can and will be tested daily.

What would happen if we lifted the heavy thing right in front of us? What if we bore our cross voluntarily?

I fumble for my mask, argue with gravity, win, and stand up.

If there had been a tiny hula dancer on the dashboard, she would have smirked as I lumber out in festive suspenders, grab a pile of books to read aloud, and head towards the door.

(In a mask-muffled tone):   "Good morning, Charlene!"

(Leaning into the new scanning thermometer).   *BEEP.*

"97.3."

"Any symptoms?"

"No"

Nausea?

"No"

Sore Throat?

"No"

"Been on a cruise in the last 14 days?"

"Ha, I wish!"

The empty hall yawns dimly before me.

It's time to work.

Josh Urban

Chapter 3 - *Days In The Hall*

The dining room is sulking, silently, dimly, alone. The weak March sky filters through the windows, gray. There's no murmured gossip about Mildred and her friend, no complaining about the soup. There's nobody to grumble. The dining room is closed.

My nicer cheap shoes pad pad pad vigorously through the silence, past the March 2020 activity calendar hanging on the bulletin board. It will be there for months, unneeded and unheeded.

Outside the window, the half-empty swimming pool lurks sullenly under a tattered cover. The lifeguard chair has been rusting for a good ten years.

One fine September evening when the chair was shiny and the building was a hotel, Ms. Val had her wedding anniversary dinner where the steakhouse used to be, down the hall.

She told me yesterday when I went to visit her in room 304. We both looked around for a moment, wistfully, slightly baffled.

The hotel walls have been converted into a retirement home, and neither of us imagined we'd be here.

Rainwater fills the pool. The steakhouse is gone, changed into the common room. Ms. Val plays bingo there. Or would.

The state has suspended group activities. She waits patiently in her room, crossing off the days on an empty calendar with a single stroke of a pencil.

Sometimes I can feel those thin graphite lines wind around my throat like a noose.

Pad pad pad down the hall. My Chinese mask smells of chemicals. *Ah, a fresh one - the new smell of morning.* My suspenders feel more chipper than I do. The access key swings around my neck, yellow, plastic, authoritative, opening any door. With authority comes responsibility – to knock. Pants are never a guaranteed answer. *Oh god...I'm a DJ – I'm not meant for this.*

The nurses are built from stronger stuff, with bulletproof noses. One of the toughest stands in gentle strength at her cart, counting out the morning medicine.

"Hey Nikki, Gooooood morning."

She looks up. Only twice have her eyes flared in frustration from behind her glasses. I don't know how she does it.

"Hey Josh, good morning."

Ms. Val leans out of her door, watchful as only an old lady can be. "Hi there. Saw your car. Are we going to have music today?"

"Oh yeah. I'll be back around noon."

Pad pad pad to the office. I move a board game and some fake flowers, clearing a space for my books.

"Morning, Marie!"

She looks up from her break, ready to head down the hall to visit residents.

"Mmm, good morning."

A laptop whirs to life, and I heave. With a metallic rattle, my DJ cart rumbles down the hall.

First Stop Second Floor

The red flatbed hand cart has been customized, turned into a mobile DJ rig. I built it between the time people were restricted and locked. Little Mrs. Beecher watched me. I let her try the circular saw. "A life's wish" she said, squealing delightedly. *Hope I don't get sued.* It roared uneventfully across the board.

The rig is made from 2x4's, a half of a table, a piece of plywood, a crate of records, a basket with all the wires, plus accouterments. A deck of cards for some magic tricks. A Bible. A magnetic sticker of Kim Kardashian crying, a leftover from the vapid pop culture days pre-pandemic. (Maturity isn't an overnight thing in my case.)

"Is that your girlfriend?" a foreign nurse asks one day.

"Ha!"

The cart rattles to a stop, parked in the hall, second floor. Millie wanders out. Millie is always wandering out. The isolation is hell on her dementia. Each week it's worse. She doesn't understand the new rules. I don't know how long she can last on the assisted living side.

She seems to need more care.

"Hi Millie, good morning. Want to hear some music? Why don't you just sit in this chair right by your door...no, no, not in the hall, right here. That's the ticket."

She complies. I start the tunes. She starts to dance to Elvis.

Joan pokes her head out. The isolation will make her crack, too. One day she tells me she has just stolen a car.

Before all this is over, she'll be on the secure memory care ward to stare her days away. Millie will join her. But we don't know that yet.

I lean over the microphone, addressing the hall.

"Annnd here's a hit from 1956. It's Fats Domino's 'Blueberry Hill!'"

The piano jumps out of the speakers, filling the hall. I hope people are listening behind closed doors. Millie and Joan, sitting in their doorways, tap their toes. It's almost normal.

(Once Beethoven was too loud, and Ms. Nelson shot into the hall to complain. That's how we met. To this day, we're good friends.)

After an hour, Louis Armstrong's "Wonderful World" drifts around, closing with a message of hope. I unplug. "Till tomorrow, ladies."

Play it again, Josh

Then it's a repeat of the show on the third floor. Then the first. Then memory care – the dementia ward. After a few weeks, it's obvious that some TVs could be fixed, and some more people talked to, and some books could be read and stories to be heard. A hundred ways to be useful flash up, blinking like beacons.

Hear me. See me. Help me.

I adjust accordingly. Weeks turn into months. The curve isn't flattened[1], but the goalposts have moved.

---

1 The "flatten the curve"campaign aimed to avoid overwhelming hospitals with a spike of infections by implementing social distancing, lockdowns, and shuttering businesses and churches. It started as "15 days to slow the spread" on March 16th, 2020, but lasted much longer. (See *Timeline, p. 8.*)

The building feels like a cruise ship, shuttered and slowly sinking. Eighty souls are declining.

The records spin 'round and round. The water keeps flooding into my mind. Sometimes it leaks out my eyes. My suspenders feel more chipper than I do.

A Hundred Times

Fats Domino has told us about Blueberry Hill a hundred times. A hundred times the cart has rumbled to a stop. A hundred times Millie has sat in her doorway and listened. Three hundred times I've reminded her to stay in her room. Fifty times she asks why.

Zero times does she understand.

Ms. Val keeps adding lines to the empty calendar, crossing out the days, that thin graphite thread strong enough to hang a man.

Summer greens the trees outside the heavy windows. Inside, life is frozen in place.

Bird Feeders

I park the cart, and start a Grieg piano concerto in the first floor hall. Ms. Abby relishes classical music.

"Reminds me of my daughter. She was a great pianist, could play all that stuff so beautifully. Cancer stole her away."

Ms. Abby fiddles with a rosary, drifting away on the key of A minor, remembering.
I pause a moment, looking at the lonely old lady's bowed head, and bow mine, too.

Moments of poignancy tumble out of every closet, every ordinary door, mingling with the rustle of scrubs as the nurses prowl the hallways. One walks by. Her radio beeps. "203 needs assistance." The reverie is broken.

The piano concerto is about a half hour long – plenty of time. I grab a small blue bucket.

"Slow down, Josh." Nikki laughs gently. "I can hear you walking when you're on the floor above."

"Really?"

"Really."

Pad pad pad down the hall, with the grace and subtlety of an elephant.

Ah well...

It's time to feed the birds.

Josh Urban

Chapter 4 - *The Bird Feeder*

The back door wooshes open, the hot breath of July arguing with a whining air conditioner. My voice adds to the tumult.

"'Sup, Tameka? I'm off to feed the birds!"

The nurse looks up from a cigarette, her kindly chuckle breaking around the edge, cracking with nicotine and fatigue. On these front lines, she's a gunner, and I'm the drummer boy.

Hopping off through the side yard, past the broken walkers and rusting junk, I can breathe freely for once in the workday.

Nobody tells me to wear a mask among the forgotten greenery.

A suspended sense of time pervades the building. It's palpable, even from the outside looking in.

After the initial ceding of the "two weeks to flatten the curve", the inch rapidly grows into a mile, then another, then another, then another, stretching out into a future that many residents know they don't posses. Only a grinding uncertainty remains.

A month's length is inversely proportional to the wrinkles around your eyes.

The bird feeders outside the windows reside permanently in the laze of a summer afternoon, focal points of a now-ness, an alternately crushing and liberating present.

Early in the lockdown, I added a few feeders to the collection, building them in my garage wood shop. Positive action became tangible, scents of cedar sawdust.

My nicer cheap shoes wind carefully through the grass. A young maple sways in the breeze. The clouds start to congregate, plotting — the planning committee of an afternoon thunderstorm.

The strip of woods in the middle of this shopping town whispers greenly, a shadow of sanity among the concrete "progress."

The residents sit inside, looking out, waiting, stuck in a prison built of fortnights.

The trees stare back. My mind wanders. Do the birds watch the people, as the people watch the birds?

Do they comment on the solitaire games of Mr. James as he keeps his bedridden wife company? Will they watch the news with Ms. Watson, or wait for the silent telephone to have mercy on Mr. Redding? Maybe Dr. Doolittle could translate their chips and chirps from Bird into English:

"Caw! Did you see that new guy jump? He walked into Mr. Simpson's room, and Mr. Simpson didn't have his pants on. Again."

"Heavens! Did he knock?" Goldfinch laughs.

"Oh yeah. But the new guy assumed pants were a given. Bet that's the last time he does that. Caw caw!"

Overhead, the planning committee takes a lunch break. The clouds part. The blaze returns. I work my way down the line of feeders.

A blue jay chases a dove away. A starling flutters down, and starts a hunt for fallen seeds. His iridescent black feathers contrast salmon legs as he ambles along, bobbing his head.

How his dinosaur ancestors would smirk, but he's a city bird, and doesn't have time for abstractions. Missing a caterpillar, he starts to gossip with Blue Jay.

"Hey Jay, I see Ms. Beauregard hasn't gotten out of bed today. What's her deal?"

"Would you?" Jay's crest fluffs up.

"She moved here just as the lockdown started. What's most important to her is in a graveyard in Texas. All she has left is a picture of him. I see her take it out from under her pillow sometimes and kiss it, ya know. Gotta be tough to be a widow. She's got his CD's —he was a drummer or tuba player or something I think. She listened to it again the other day."

Starling settles in to listen. Jay's on a roll.

"Only made her feel half bad. But all those buttons on the stereo are hard to see, and the wrong one always gets pushed. And if you wanna talk about buttons: the numbers on the phone look so blurry.

She tries to call her daughter when she's sad, but can never remember to dial 9 first, and it all takes too long. The line goes dead. She gives up if she gets up, so sometimes she doesn't."

At the shadow of a hawk, or maybe just the suspicion of danger, they flit away, their conversation another sacrifice to the ravenous god of Safety.

The maple stirs again, and the dove returns to a feeder, gentle and humble. I watch her watching, and continuing the daydream, imagine her thoughts:

She glances in the office window. *Is that a white cardigan on the boss's chair?* Although strange for July, Dove knows that Cold isn't as simple as a seasonality.

She keeps her tiny black eye trained on the window. She sees head nurses and their lieutenants, telling, always telling. Some of their faces have become twisted and hard, like the foxes in the woods. Dove sees cages in their eyes.

That one likes to point her finger often. She seems to be doing it a lot more these past few months. She seems to be...enjoying it.

Then Dove hears Jay and Starling arguing about sunflower seeds, and flies off to better things. Her chicks are waiting. Squeaky wings beat a rhythm in the heavy summer air.

High above the baking earth, the planning committee resumes deliberations. There *would* be a storm.

I bustle back inside, empty bird food bucket swinging.

"See ya around, Tameka." My voice is muffled. "Off to some hallway bingo!"

Her smoky laugh bounces off the closing back door.

I smile under my mask.

◆▷

Hallway Snapshot: Twinning

Nurse Tameka, muffled in a knock off Gucci mask.
"A guy up on Lincoln Ave has a stand."
"Oh, that is so here!"
My gallows laugh is harshly sincere.
She brings me one next week.
Give me a cigarette and a bayonet
Send me out to Flanders or anywhere
If I get to serve with this battalion.
We'll be icons in the trenches.
Twinning.

◆▷

Hallway Snapshot: Nineteen Rounds

———————

If a prize fighter's eyes shout diesel and blood
Hers
Whisper past lives
Of deer and ferns

Today they're glazed above her uniform
Activity Department Green.

"Connie, are you alright? You're listing to one side."

"I called nineteen rounds of hallway bingo…Nineteen rounds, Josh. I kept
them entertained."

The bell rings. Do we answer?

I've tried to drown its shrill a thousand times
With a swimming pool of excuses
And a turn of the pillow to the cold side

Or a shuffling of paperwork in the safety of my office
Or anywhere
Outside the ring.
Somebody raise her hand.
Champion.

Josh Urban

Chapter 5 - *Hello, Chuck!*

Ding! The elevator doors slide open on the third floor. *Heave!* The rumble of the music cart breaks the 23 hour silence.

A nurse looks up from her phone, then back down, still bored.

Just press Play. The dreary corridor turns into a scrapbook of audio memories. On this floor, the first song is always the same: Benny Goodman's "Stompin' at the Savoy." It's a time machine from 1936.

The song purrs of golden nights faded into sepia photographs, laughter with a crinkle cut edge.

A slight crackle of dust on the record, the trombones murmur warmly, a sparkling trumpet concurs. Benny's bespectacled opinions float through in mellow tones. With attention, you can hear the ghosts of June evenings flit past. Where did that time go? The river flows unceasingly, and we find ourselves far downstream.

Where are the dancers?

One of them wheels his way to the door, stopping before the forbidden hall. He looks up.

"Hello, Chuck! Want a soda?"

"Sure, Coach, that would be great!"

The old man's deep-set brown eyes gleam with friendly recognition. He reaches up from his wheelchair with the offering, a guy's guy host in a polo shirt and khaki shorts.

It's been hard for him to carry on his natural brand of North Carolina hospitality cooped up in the old hotel room. But, the human spirit is stronger than the CDC. He finds a way to retain a bit of humanity through generosity. He gives what he has. In this case, it's a few generic colas squirreled away in the mini-fridge.

The top pops. I plop down in a chair. Our new tradition continues. It's about 11:30 on a Tuesday, a carbon-copy of Monday. Wednesday promises a triplicate, indefinitely.

The hall eats calendars for breakfast.

My name isn't Chuck. But, masks put voices beyond the reach of hearing aids. Josh was transposed.

His name isn't Coach. It's Jim. "Moved here from Carolina in '61. Thought I'd just be here for two years...and stayed." The 1962 football season at Wilson High earned him the name.

He must have been good. The phone, cranked so his ninety one year old ears can hear it, blares. "One of my players calling to say hello."

Upon his return, Coach's eyes sparkle, his face starts to beam. Something goes endearingly funny with his mouth. He chomps down.

It appears as if he's bitten into an especially tasty sour candy, fruits of a life well-lived, trying to be modest, his smile unquenchable anyway.

There we sit, two men with new names, listening to music for a spell each morning, pandemic pals, brothers in arms, floating away on the sound of big band.

A Free Vacation

"The soda tastes extra good today. Thanks, Coach, I sure was thirsty."

Getting to know someone takes time, but we have plenty here on the third floor. War stories blend with the mundane.

Repetition of a theme, a gradual introduction of something new, an occasional kicker to make my head spin. Benny Goodman would call it music.

Today, my game is off. "What's the farthest you've traveled?"

"North Korea" he shoots back.

"Oh yeah."

Silence, then… "I never want to see a mountain again."

Patsy Cline walks after midnight, and fills the hush we sit in. He had told me some, but never about anything grisly.

Wikipedia said it rained a lot, so there would have been mud.

Lots of mud, and the killing. Do ends justify means? What about in a trench? Easy for me to wax philosophical and flatten any nuance out of it, warm and dry as I am.

Dark wings rustle in a wind of Ignorance, Ruin flying at the speed of our Forgetfulness.

"You ever hear of Heartbreak Ridge and Pork Chop Hill?" Coach had asked the first time we talked, looking up with sharp eyes.

Unacceptable ignorance arrived in a sudden flush. I hadn't, but mumbled my way out of it.

He chose not to notice.

Today, he tells a bit more.

"It was just like the movies. We fought at night, and slept during the day. You could hear them talking, that's how close the enemy was. One day, sleeping in a bunker made of sandbags, I wake up to my buddies yelling "SIBLEY! SIBLEY! GET OUTTA THERE!"

His eyes bug out. He waves his arms.

"An attack?" I lean forward in my chair.

"A mudslide. The sandbags started to fall, and the only thing that kept me from being crushed was a lone tent pole!"

"Woah." We both lean back in silence, thinking.

I speak first. "Geeze, that woulda sucked being killed like that!"

"Yeah, yeah, I guess it would have!" He breaks into a rare laugh.

Life in the Key of Ding

Another day, another elevator ding, another spin of Stompin' at the Savoy at 11:20 am.

Another chipping away, front porch stories set against the monotony of the forbidden hall.

The bad doctor, the death of his father, the struggles of his mother, the crushing poverty, the old-fashioned mule-instead-of-tractor stepdad, the pickle factory, the love of sports, the war, raising two kids, golf, mutual funds, church...A detail here, an anecdote there as Benny plays the clarinet in the background, and Elvis is all shook up.

"I taught driving school in the 70's."

"Of course." The fit is archetypal.

He told me the story of how he met her the second time we talked, but he tells it again today.

It was a warm spring night in North Carolina, and two friends were heading to the basketball game. Their lady friend, a third, needed a gentleman to accompany her. Would he round out the quartet?

"Sure, I'll take her!" He waves his arm from his wheelchair, young again.

The dice of fortune have that effect, even in the retelling of a toss.

"I didn't know her, but I said I'd take her. Her name was Lily."

He puts his arm down, suddenly old again.

"You have a picture of her?"

"No, not here...somewhere. She sure was pretty."

I rise. It's time to play *her song*. Nobody talks. Nat King Cole's "Unforgettable" fills the air. I know to look at the floor by now.

He gets misty-eyed every time.

The date had worked. He had danced with her, married her, raised two children with her, grown old with her.

To his great sadness, he's outlived her.

Every day, when the music is done, he wheels alone back to his chair. I can hear the numbing TV, and he sits, wistfully looking out over the parking lot. A piece of him is gone, and while the song plays, I bleed with him.

July 12th

"August 15th."

"What's that?" I'm kicked back in the chair, drumming a finger to Glenn Miller's beat on the speakers. The fine July morning hums outside the plate glass windows. Inside, it's business as usual.

"Lily's birthday."

"Oh." I raise my eyebrows slightly over the generic cola can, making a mental note.

Later I email his son. "Hey Nate, got an idea."

Nate sends what's needed. It's perfect.

August 15th

The day rolls around, like it always does. August 15th.

11:20 am. Ding! The nurse looks up, and back down, still bored. The DJ cart rumbles across the floor. Benny Goodman starts the band.

"Hello, Chuck!"

"Coach, I got something for ya. It's Lily's birthday, right?"

The old man's eyes widen, drawn to the framed photo, riveted. It's Lily at 19, the year they met. Her dark hair is radiant against the optimistic skin of youth.

Blue eyes pierce the glass, reaching across years to this hall that's locked and empty, where masks hide and choke, where names are obscured and patience is the virtue, to the old man bravely carrying on.

She would be so proud of her hero.
Maybe her eyes send a simple "I love you". They say something.

He trembles. His mouth opens, quavers, and lets out a half-choked cry.

His brown eyes start to well.

My shoes beeline for the door. We both need a moment.

Neither of us know he's only got two months left to miss her.

I have an inkling that "Stompin' at the Savoy" will make me think of him someday soon.

Whenever I listen close to the golden murmur of trombones on a dusty record, I can almost hear them dancing.

Josh Urban

◀▷

Hallway Snapshot: Uncrumpled

———

A priceless gem
Two feet and a gas pedal
On a sunny Sabbath
"Sure is gonna be lonesome 'round here without you"
"I'll be back Monday, Coach, and bring you some stories."

The door begrudged me
Three months nearly broke me

But
The mountain road gained
My mind uncrumpled
Like aluminum foil
Tiny wrinkles
Still behind my eyes
As they drink in
Ancient granite and
An alpine breeze indifferent to Madness.

Chapter 6 - **North Woods**

Is Peace found, or created? Is it to be hoped upon, prayed for, washed up by chance on a serene beach, shining in the absence of conflict? Or is it forged in the crucible of the Everyday, wrought from the 9-5 and ten thousand settings of the table?

We all hold the old lady with white hair in high regard. She moves slowly, but consistently, a measured tranquility and pastel colors, walking to the side of the hall.

Slower Traffic Keep Right.

She thinks before she talks. There's a bit of the North Woods in her, a bracing ice tinged with spruce, a bloodline of snow and alpine summers.

A hand-drawn sign in Crayola blue hangs on her open door. *One Day at a Time*. I heed the advice, breaking my stride from the usual manic run.

Knock, knock , knock.

"Gertie, have time for a quick chat?"

She lowers an Amish romance novel, her clear gray eyes rising from the page to my face, affixing fully - and then replies.

"Sure."

"May I sit?"

"Oh yes."

The rocker has a doorman. I move the Chicago Cubs hat (Gertie loves baseball) from the vintage doll's head, and then Dolly herself. One of three keepsakes in the spartan room, she deserves extra care.

The game isn't on TV today. Good. I won't have to fake knowing what's happening with the Packers or the Cubs. It never works, anyway.

The cool maintenance guys trail off anytime I try to join the sports talk. An old lady changing the subject to something more understandable is ten times as humbling.

The rocker creaks. Huffing and puffing through the mask, I sit, winded from my rounds. It's not that I want to run. Scores of friends are frozen in isolation, and the faster my feet, the more I can try to thaw...before it's too late.

Maybe a passenger train locomotive feels the same. In temporary rest, it waits, steaming and whirring at the platform, an eye for the red signal to blink to green, ready to roar on down the hall.

The challenge is to snap focus – be present now, run in five minutes, arrive at the next station with a hurried knock and bellowed "HELLO, MR. SMITH!" Operatic breath support. Yell from the diaphragm to project through a mask. Repeat.

Gertie eyes me, waiting for the calm.

"How have you been?"

"Chopped some firewood today." My morning chores recall the past for her. She begins.

"Dad would hitch up a team of horses, and drag trees out of the snowy Wisconsin forests to keep us warm. The power company didn't want to run the line an extra mile for one customer, so we used oil lamps, too," she reminisces.

"That's crazy, man!"

"Oh, we liked it fine. The wood stove kept us plenty warm" she replies in a Bluebird Wisconsin accent, round and musical. Her neutral face could be mistaken for blank. A slower look reveals an honest mirror.

It reminds me of a deep pool in a
mountain stream, unruffled, shining the true
nature of the matter back with quiet observation.
Today, it reflects a hint of my modern softness.

I shift slightly. The antique rocker creaks.

Intentions

The rooms at Statler Place are identical.
The former hotel is an inadvertent social
experiment if you know how to look: *What do
people do with what they have?*

Some rooms are hospital bare, others
stuffed with heavy furniture that follows
owners like a mahogany ball and chain from the
Better Days. Bottle the murky air and sell it as
Melancholia—the Cologne.

Hers, in contrast, is tidy, sunny, and claimed.

I compliment it today, thinking Gertie's actions are making the best of a bad deal.

After all, a lady moved in this morning — unwillingly—and caused a scene. Ms. Maria's venom is fresh in my mind: The insisted treachery of her daughter, the prompt threat to hang herself...(she didn't). Ms. Maria is new, and this is on the dramatic side of adjusting, but still...the lockdowns.

Who would want this?

The mirror face scrunches in disagreement at the implied misfortune.

"Oh no, I'm glad to be here. My kids were afraid to ask me if I'd like to come, and I said "About time!" I've got everything I want, and I'm content with my friends, doing my crosswords, reading my books, watching the birds...I need to be here, and this is perfect."

The sun streams through the window, setting her white hair ablaze. I rock back slightly, impressed.

Her peace is forged, intentional. Like her father eighty years before, she has hacked out a home in the midst of a wilderness, and prospered.

It wasn't easy.

Keeping Promises

The vow Gertie made to John sixty years
ago was witnessed at their Methodist church.
The kids grew up and moved out. Her word was
stronger than his Alzheimer's. They got a room
on the dementia ward where Hell is quantified.

Instead of an altimeter, the Global
Deterioration Scale measures this descent,
inevitably backwards from dignity to diapers.
If one is lucky, the reaper takes you out before
Level 7, a state of infancy.

Benjamin Button is your neighbor,
screaming in the hall at three in the morning.

"Are the kids ready for school? I want to
go home! Why won't you let me go home?"

What do you do in Hell? How do you act properly? We young(er) people often exorcise the inevitable future with a saccharine "I love old people" and a quick glance at our phone, a blessed distraction of hip culture that never dies. *That won't be us. That's for old people.*

Forget chances—we act like there's a *choice* of bad weather.

The storm wasn't optional for Gertie. The winds howled, and the rain beat down.

She chose to stand up and be decent, a simple act of utmost bravery.

She lived with her husband in those halls of delirium knowing only she would return. Ghosts need friends too. She became a Rock of the Ordinary to everyone on the ward.

Books provided the occasional respite. Long before the lockdowns, Gertie came to a program "on the normal side", and borrowed a volume on guitars. I was confused. I thought she was in Memory Care. No, she was just being a good nurse. Some people never retire. Some people are unbreakable.

With the promise fulfilled, and John finally at mercy, she moved back downstairs to Assisted Living. She was sad. She mourned.

Although weighed by the stone of grief, at her command, her feet moved forward. The sunny glade of her new life wasn't cleared by a thudding ax, but by a baby blue crayon over ordinary paper, blindingly white in the crushing Present.

One Day at a Time.

Long Walks

"What would you like to hear, Gertie?"
Between the hard quarantines, the dining room
would occasionally reopen. When it did, I'd
DJ lunch. We all loved requests and their
accompanying stories.

"How about Sentimental Journey? It was
my nursing class's graduating song."

One day when I swooped by her table for
a new suggestion, she pulled out her phone and
showed me an app.

"Look at this—I've got a little tracker.
My room is so far at the end of hall, that if I
come to three meals, and bingo...I walk a mile!"

Over the next few days, she'd proudly let me know if she hit her goal. Then the next round of (questionable) PCR tests came back positive. You'll find what you're looking for.

We plunged back into the lonely waters of another quarantine.

Prison Workouts

The One Day at a Time sign still hangs, but the door is closed, per regulations. I've got an isolation gown on. According to the rules, that makes it OK to visit.

Knock, knock, knock.

"How are you, Gertie?"

Move the antique doll. Slow down.

"I'm good, Josh. I walked a mile yesterday."

"How?! They aren't letting people out." The mask can't stifle my surprise.

"I did laps right here in my room."

"Gertie..that's like a prison workout. Rock on."

"Yeah, well..." Her quiet chuckle is the laugh of a mountain brook that's been carving stone for a long, long time.

"Some things just have to be done."

Chapter 7 - *St. Anthony's*

"And his name was Tony Fauci."

The mask holds my jaw up.

"It was *not!*"

Being offended, clutching a Bible, and lacking a snappy comeback are three things alien to me.

Don's not in his right mind. Yet he's managed to capture the spirit of the times, blurt it out—and level me. The second floor dementia ward (memory care) has a knack for it.

Good Morning, Vietnam

The day is gray outside the tinted windows. Good. It's worse when it's a clear blue sky. To starve of Life is bad enough without taunting sunbeams.

I put the stack of books on the table, careful to avoid the juice marks.

Twenty-odd ghosts drift about the ward. Some patients are a touch off, others sit immobile.

The unrelenting clock of Dementia ticks louder in some, but is heard in all.

It never goes backwards, only down.

Little Mrs. Andrews watches the birds out the window wistfully.

"Look at them...Five today."

The geese have it made: free, breathing the suburban air, piney fresh by comparison. Their webbed feet pad over asphalt, silent outside of locked windows.

Paternity king Maury crows at the suffering Young on the TV.

"Oh, so you're not the daddy!"

The suffering Old sit in a stupor, grimy sheets covering the couches, not knowing their daddy, either.

The ward needs more lights. Or, for Bill, head of facilities, to stop turning them off. But who's to know? The Health Department isn't letting families inside.

Strangely enough, twenty odd ghosts are less affected by the lockdowns than any other floor.

Memory Care is always quarantined. It's a secure floor on the best of days. A lady who thinks it's 1965 will absentmindedly brush away a mask, and the unceasing wandering is a common part of the disease.

They cluster together, huddling in each other's company, a crowded bus stop in a heavy fog.

Phrases like "social distancing" hold as much weight as "collateral damage" does. They don't understand directions or euphemisms—or forget them. But they miss their families. That line to reality is severed. Confusion closes in faster.

What if they test positive for COVID? A case with symptoms, a case without, and a possible false positive are all treated the same.

An unused ward serves as an isolation wing for the entire building. They're shipped there for two long, silent weeks, with only an occasional nurse for human connection.

I survey the dismal scene. Mustering the air—and the will—for the volume required...

"GOOD MORNING!"

"Good morning, dear."

A tiny lady with a southern accent totters up, clutching a purse. It's Millie. Nursing moved her over last week. Patsy Cline records each day on the Assisted Living side couldn't keep her afloat. The isolation became too heavy.

"My son will help me."

"Your son isn't allowed to visit right now. Hopefully soon..."

Here she is, wondering where she is.

"Now, what is your name again?"

"JOSH. I'm JOSH."

"Oh, thank you, dear."

My feet stir, remembering, restless, moving, always moving. I'm here to help, and paid to do so.

But it's hard.

The Water Boy

I called mom after work yesterday. "I feel like a water boy in Hell. What do you bring to people who are burning?"

The clock is merciless, always forward, tick tock.

Why do the beats sound like the crackle of flames sometimes? There's no time to sit on a mountain and think up a solution.

Action is demanded now. I pull up the cleanest chair I can find.

"Who wants to hear some stories?"

A kindly nurse helps them shuffle over.

"Josh is reading now. Let's listen to Josh reading. Come on, Mr. Don."

This ghost is new. He's in the early stages of the disease.

Save the Whales

Don's affliction is of a singular
cruelty. He used to be brilliant, distinguished,
internationally-known. Now he's here. I'm
reminded of a rusting Corvette anytime we speak.

His preposterous claims are often based
in truth, natural intelligence shining through his
suffering. Don was once a colleague of Anthony
Fauci's. (I looked it up.) His stories of the Navy
rescuing the "three remaining whales in the
world" give my jaded eyebrows a raise, but aren't
out of line with the illness.

Dementia has an unsettling way of
breaking off chunks of truth in the sufferer's
brain. Although the context might be scrambled,
it's not always random.

Old mothers fret about their kids being late for school. Elderly men look for the bus stop forty years too late.

Don's whale story, repeated often, makes sense to me. He would have been involved in important projects in the past. And he listens to a lot of news.

Don pulled me aside last week, face dark with suspicion. With a whisper, he alleged that Jane, another patient, was "stealing puppies and drowning them in the lake."

He wanted me to do something.

It took a few days before the idea buzzed to my mind, like a beagle-hungry sand fly. Somehow the news had briefly surfaced, to be briefly inquired about.

Don's old colleague, Fauci, had been accused of signing off on the experiments with ravenous flies and puppies eaten alive.

My God. What rusty razor blade had broken off in Don's brain?

I hoped the real news and his delusions had no relation, that he had no reason to know.

He seemed pleasant enough. Then again, so do most people. Oh, they wouldn't hurt a fly. But a fly would hurt a beagle. Would Don?

Why do we always assume we'd be the hero of history if only we were there to save the day? How many of us would be holding the match?

The times rattle my cage again.

John 1

I push the thoughts aside. There's reading to do. A few stories, then the Bible. I shake my head inwardly. How things change. Three years ago I was a militant agnostic.

Casual ignorance casts ugly shadows in the firelight of the Present. The way forward is murky. I'm certain of less – except that these words insist on being aired here, now.

Mr. James surfaced at yesterday's reading. He recited half his favorite psalm in his deacon's voice, rusty from the years.

"The Lord is my shepherd, I shall not want."

Everyone chimed in. We got through the words, and perhaps something else.

I flip to the Gospel of John. The beginning is a good place to start. With clear a voice as I can muster through the mask:

"In the beginning was the Word, and the Word was with God, and the Word was God. The same was in the beginning with God. All things were made by him; and without him was not any thing made that was made. In him was life; and the life was the light of men. And the light shineth in darkness; and the darkness comprehended it not."

The room is still, listening. Maury is carrying on dimly in the background. These words cut through the fetid air, knives of truth. I'm vaguely aware of a tear in my eye. I'm not sure why.

I continue.

"There was a man sent from God, whose name...."

Don breaks in with a dementia laugh.

"And his name was Tony Fauci."

Cities on a Hill

◀▷

Hallway Snapshot: The Cooler

"March '21 Notice to the families: Any resident who leaves for Easter will need to quarantine for 14 days upon their return, regardless of COVID status. Memory care patients who are unable to stay in their rooms will be housed in Third Floor West to avoid exposing others to danger. This additional expense will be added to their bills." - MGMT

A positive test
Might be false
Might be true
Either way
It's a ticket to the Cooler
No symptoms are no exemption
Never mind the error rate of the PCR
Extra space on a wing nobody sees
They open sometimes when needed
For you to get better

Cities on a Hill

Up on Third Floor West
A more complete bubble
It's quiet as Death
The stacked wheelchairs
Unused

One nurse checks in
to see how you're bobbing
in the ocean
The whirlpool where the waters of
Theory and Practice collide
Can drag a man down as he contemplates
an empty wall
for two long weeks
Stay home, stay safe
Stay sane.

Josh Urban

Hallway Snapshot: Lists

Shirley likes making lists
At the morning staff meetings
Her careful script
curls in benign dry erase
Outlines who's the most lonely
and could use a room visit

Soon most of the residents
names are written
With squiggly stars next to their room numbers

Top Priority

I start to raise a boss's hand
With a plastic cuff
To explain that's not how priorities work

And realize it's mine that don't.
Everyone is the most lonely.

Shirley adds another star.

Chapter 8 - *Chapters At An Exhibition*

"Any chills, body aches?"

Charlene's job is to ask, so she does, every day. The training manual says the front desk is the first line of defense. It was written when the balance of power between the colored tabs and sanity was stable.

There's the knot in my stomach. It gurgles at what they're doing to us. It tightens at the realization that we're letting them. It's a different kind of sick.

"Any nausea, vomiting?"

"No."

It's been months of her asking. The only thing different about today is the guitar on my back. Soon I'm on the third floor to entertain the residents.

"This one goes out to the governor and his extended lockdowns."

I perch on the edge of a chair, cradling the acoustic, trying not to crush it with a vicious clamp of my arm. How fragile it seems. How fragile everything seems.

Coach sits in his doorway, brown eyes watching above his mask.

The twang makes a feeble echo against the blank face of the hall. I start in on "Folsom Prison Blues."

He chuckles, patient with this dubious Johnny Cash rendition, so I continue.

The sound drifts further on down the line. I follow it with my eyes. It reflects in the emptiness.

Sam's door is propped open a crack. The sound wanders in. He doesn't come out.

Sam is as ancient, and as young, as a gnarled oak in the spring. He's become another adopted grandfather to me. I hope he doesn't die soon. I hope he doesn't die ever.

Ooo, that one's gonna hurt.

Now they're taking his time. How much does he have left? My fragile guitar is glad I try to forget about it.

Perhaps he's watching a movie, halfway through a giant box of DVD's from Doris—the second time. *Will they ever make a show about this mess?*

Maybe I should write a song about it. Could a wailing blues guitar ever capture this anguish and hopelessness—and the mind-numbing boredom?

The chords I play are familiar. My mind wanders on autopilot.

In 1874, Modest Moussorgsky composed "Pictures at an Exhibition".

It was a work of grief, a memorial
to the artist friend who had died suddenly.
Moussorgsky helped stage a posthumous art
show, visited it, and later, when his tears dried,
wrote the paintings into sound.

What if Sam were a series of pictures,
too? What would they look like? Perhaps...

The Old Boat, Summer Afternoon, Oil on Canvas

Sam is not an old boat. But sometimes he
sits like one, pulled up in the reeds, gently musing
on the end of summer. Subdued oils blend onto
the canvas. Tans, greens, a faded blue overhead,
humid, muted. The planks of the watercraft
are as white as his hair, and speak of gallantry,
storms, sunrises and sets, swells in the endless
blue.

Now it's glad to sit and talk quietly with the lapping waves. The slanting sun catches their crests, twinkling like his kind eye as the water-men rush past, off to greet the important schooners blustering into port with billowing sails.

In the distance, an ancient building dips its feet to the briny water and remembers summers past, "FISK'S SHELLFISH" emblazoned in peeling letters. High overhead, God is a baker, kneading the flour of September clouds into the morrow's daily bread.

Unpaintable is the smell of sweet autumn clematis, the scent of Forever on a late summer's afternoon. Somewhere, there's an echo of the laughter at high noon, gone on like the tide. Or maybe it's just a seagull. Sam is not an old boat. But he could be.

Dance at the National Convention of the Tall Club, Oil on Canvas

The gilded frame is wedding-band gold. The scene is formal, important. A fine young man leans his great height forward in a bow. "May I have this dance?" A fine young woman curtsies. She's tall, too. So are the onlookers, faces dim in the rich dark colors. Rembrandt would have approved of the play of light and shadow, a glow surrounding the couple.

Although their real meeting at the Tall Club occurred in an era of postwar pastel, the gravity of the scene deserves the Dutch treatment. The artist was correct in using his best paints. The scene would endure till death did they part.

After two years of long-distance courtship, Sam turned to Margaret and said "You know, I think I'd like to marry you." She looked at him. "You know, I think I'd like that."

Hallway Bingo, Oil on Canvas

These colors are slashed and smeared into a modern ashcan style, their hues vibrantly aching in the trial of another day. Old folk lean out of their rooms into the dim hall. The dark chestnut of the vinyl wood flooring catches an occasional glint from the brilliant window at the end, unattainable.

The nurse's green top and khaki pants end in the surprise of pink crocs.

Connie from Activities looks tired as she pushes a cart, bravely. Taking a seat, she picks up a microphone, enunciating through her blue mask.

"B...11. That's BEE ONE ONE."

Sam leans forward towards the empty chair facing him, scanning the green and red bingo cards streaked in a weary stroke of the brush.

Nothing.

The Locking of the Sun, Oil on Wood

Browns, blacks, and a hint of maroon sit flat on the board, matching the flat voice of the thin young man with a haggard face.

His hand, with an unearned authority, knocks, then rests on the metal door frame. An old man with white hair leans out.

"There's been another positive case, Sam. The third floor is under quarantine. I'm so sorry...we can't go outside."

"Oh. For how long?"

"Two weeks if the next round of tests clears."

The old man bows his head. In the room behind him, a crucifix hangs over a bowl of fruit. Jesus, unmasked, looks on. Nobody can meet his piercing gaze.

The Patio, Watercolor

The small painting of animals is hopeful and airy. The sun has been allowed back.

The tortoise looks up. The hummingbird in red suspenders pauses for a moment, deft wings blending into the paper.

The tortoise leans his gnarled head to one side, and says slowly "Do you know why I move my chair to the south side of the deck?"

The tortoise loves the sun, and he thinks a little joke would be good for his stressed young friend.

The hummingbird folds his wings, scratches his mask, and tries to lean into the slower pace. "Uh..no."

"Because it's closer to the sun!"

The tortoise chuckles, and relaxes into a bask. Overhead, the sun smiles, an antique lemon drop from the corner store in better days.

Spring by the Brook, Oil on Canvas

The final painting on the wall is a grand landscape. A mighty oak stands by a stream, resplendent in early spring. The winter snows have made the waters rush clear, although the skies in the distance are unsettled.

A traveler pauses on a weary journey, marveling at the sight. He doffs his cap to the tree, wondering if their places were switched, how he might grow blighted leaves and a bitter fruit for the severity of the past storms.

Yet in a quiet miracle, the ancient tree unfurls fresh green leaves in the spring breeze, smiling.

Back in Folsom Prison

Finishing my reverie, the song winds to a close. Our blues remains.

I put my guitar away, and walk down the hall.

It's almost lunchtime.

Hallway Snapshots: In Sickness and in Health

The tough love Sun
Mocked our stumbles in
High Definition Crystalline
Surround sound in our heads
Inescapable, accurate, a flashlight and a mirror
Forged into a cruel razor to leave us cut and shaking
Until Nurse Cindy banished it with a flick of the wrist
On the cord of the blinds
And we settled in to watch
A respite of faded color

Six dishes at Thanksgiving
Scratchy Easter suits in 1972, The Latest Fashion
Baby tossing red and green wrapping on his
First Christmas of many, many, many
Sepia heatwaves at the merry-go-round
The music of the carnival is vanished
Silent
Missing
Drifted away

Cities on a Hill

All that's left is the rattle of this time machine
Where has it gone?
On the swells of a Pacific summer's past my dear

With Kodachrome sands of time
If we cast a line back to catch a few grains
We find them always golden

The leading lady watched
Herself on the flickering screen
Leaned over to her co-star
Who couldn't talk much
But was probably seeing all this
"Remember that, Eddie? Atlanta? And your new uniform?"
His old 8mm projector
Still working like a champ
Clickety clack
In the darkened room.
I reach up, and changed the reel.
"Want to see another, Mrs. Nelson?"
"Do you have time?"
"Sure. This one's called "So That's How It's Done".

Josh Urban

Chapter 9 - *Three Lunches*

Lunch 1

The hall is empty. A wave of my arm.

"The coast is clear. Quick!"

She zooms forward in her motorized wheelchair, the same one that ran over the executive director's foot at resident council—on purpose.

Ms. Burnside is not to be trifled with.

We're on fairly good terms now. This is after the dressing down at bingo, but before she would throw me out of her room.

I had it coming in that case. Life Rule #426:

Don't start arguments with old ladies on behalf of a teammate. It's not gentlemanly. And they'll always win.

The fresh air greets our ravenous faces. In a forgotten corner of packed dirt, sheer walls, crooked sidewalks and uncertain fences, we breathe deeply.

The world still exists.

She talks about her farm from long ago.

With an ear to the past, and an eye to the present, I balance the lunch containers on my knees, grilled cheese and a side salad.

"You'll never believe it, Ms. Burnside. A snapping turtle laid eggs in my front garden today. I put up a little fence to keep the foxes out."

She's tickled to hear the news. Anything Good is a spark in the gathering dusk. Nietzsche's madman's lantern is lit in the morning, necessary when night is continually closing in.

What is happening?

After about three of these meals, we're busted.

The outdoor lunches stop.

She keeps asking if I've seen any little snapping turtles. I haven't.

Lunch 2

If inanimate objects could think, the sign was having a Monday. Curled around it's reasonable edges, it might have grumbled:

What have I done to deserve this? I've followed orders, like the man who put me up, what's-his-face Mr. Facilities Director. HE likes telling people what to do, sending old ladies back to their room or else. The State loves telling him what to do. They push him around with the threat of fines, and don't even give a phone number to call. But here I am, no longer a superstar. There's a million of me. And I'm curling – curling! The indignity...

The sign loved telling the staff what to do, too. It ran in the growing family.

Uptight aunt signs read *Only Two People at a Time on This Elevator.*

Thuggish cousins sneered at the front counter, reminding people not to lean. *Hey, don't make it a hotspot, capiche?*

Sister signs visited from their government jobs, models washing their hands in sensible, sterile beauty. Little brother signs paid attention in first grade, learning their primary and secondary colors in big blocks of green and red and yellow. *Red Zone: Hospital gowns today, rabbit feet tomorrow, and always, always use a mask.*

Tough teenage signs earned their keep on the front door, buffeted by the wind from the real world: a reminder to read the rules and other signs.

Once limited visits started, new ones appeared just for the occasion: *Visitors are not permitted to use the public bathrooms.*

But this sign is reasonable, one of first families and founding reminders.

Please Make Sure Door Is Locked Behind You.

Even through grumbles, the sign knows it's liked. It hangs on the break room door.

Inside

The sign rustles, heeded. The door clicks shut behind me.

"Hey Josh, got your grilled cheese, I see."

"Oh hey, Tameka, how are ya? Yep, yep, my prize."

Lee Lawrie sculpted an Atlas in 1937. The bronze Greek Titan holds the celestial sphere on his shoulders outside the Rockefeller center in New York City.

Tameka is not a Greek Titan. But, if Lawrie were to fashion an Atlas of Statler Place, she would be an ideal model.

She has that nurse strength, endurance to work a double shift at the drop of a hat, go home to her kids, and refill the soap dispenser after they had used it all on mad science.

"My son keeps trying to make slime – he saw it on YouTube" she sighs as her radio beeps.

214 needs assistance.

Rising to her feet, she heads off to change someone.

The door bangs open. The sign doesn't dare protest.

Marco saunters in, Yankees cap impeccable, perched atop a fresh haircut. Gabriela, giggling, looks up adoringly, a foot and a half difference between them.

They should be Mr. and Miss Statler place, but they're not.

Hunching over the grilled cheese, I wish I was cool, and from the hood in the Bronx, with fresh kicks and tattoos that told a story of redemption and knew how to make the nurses laugh as they hold up the sky.

I also wish there wasn't COVID, and that I was a little bit taller.

Maybe I'm Ned Flanders in the room even without referencing Skee-Lo, but their smiles are contagious.

"Hey y'all!"

"Joshie Josh!" Turning back, he finishes an inside joke. Gabriela loves it.

It's said that war brings out the worst and best in people, and the worst and best people. Hard times seem to do the same. There's been a lot of corruption, poison, and reasons to lose faith.

But then there's the people like Tameka, Marco, and Gabriela, and that's reason enough to continue. They hold up the sky, or at least keep the TVs fixed and the residents cared for.

Every day, no matter what. The halls feel like trenches sometimes, and smell like them, too.

There's people to save. They love them, and they're loved back.

Contemplating the griddle mark on the last half of the grilled cheese, I listen to the banter, proud to know 'em.

Finishing, tossing trash, I heed the sign. The door locks behind me.

Back to it.

Lunch 3

"MaHAILya Jackson" she corrects, but the frost seems to be melting.

"I used to sing gospel on the radio, you know."

Ms. Washington is as prim as her dress. I am not. But we've been getting along.

She pulled out her wallet last Thursday, and furtively, without explanation, showed me a photo of her government days. She was standing next to Bill Clinton.

The DJ cart is parked up the hall. The other two ladies in their doorways hum along to the sounds of Ms. Jackson's soulful voice. It's a new lunchtime ritual.

He's got the whole world...in his hands...

Traffic flows around my chair in the hall. I'm squarely in the way, and enjoying it. Marco saunters by on the way to fix another TV. I follow him down the hall.

"Be right back, ladies."

The nurses had asked for a hand. "Ms. Washington isn't eating. She trusts you. Think you can help?"

I return with a sandwich.

"Ms. Washington, I brought you a snack. Let's eat lunch together."

She eyes the peanut butter and jelly, then me. She takes it, watching, watching. I pretend not to notice, tucking into another grilled cheese. Dean Martin's voice floats by, singing of pizza pies and *Amore*.

Ms. Washington nibbles a corner.

Ms. Val sways to the tune in her doorway, then leans forward, confidentially.

"You know, sometimes I miss Ocean City."

"Yeah?"

"Yeah...but I guess I should be here."

"Well, it's nice having you around."

There's not much for her to do except settle back in her spartan dining room chair and listen to Dean Martin.

Crash. Ms. Burnside knows how to make an entrance, even if she can't leave.

She barges to her door on my left, squinting. "My eye is worse today. OH, your ice cream."

She mashes the controls of her motorized wheelchair, spins around, slams the footrest into the wall, deepening the gash in the plaster, then disappears.

Returning, she passes out a few little cups of sugar free ice cream she's saved.

Sometimes it's chips. Once, apparently, it was Advil, and that was a problem, but today we're good. I never realized how important hosting is —the opportunity to be generous, nurturing, thoughtful, productive, *human.*

Across the way, Ms. Washington has managed a whole corner of the sandwich. Up the hall, the DJ cart continues. Frank Sinatra sings about fidelity. Nobody raises an eyebrow.

With a spring to my feet:

"Let's sing a song all together – another Mahilia Jackson. Help me if I get pitchy, OK, Ms. Washington?"

She looks up, still clutching half a sandwich, and suddenly laughs.

Press Play.

Running along the hall, waving my arms.

Everyone sings.

We shall overcome...some day....

Hallway Snapshot:
Take That Damn Mask Off

"Knof, Knof!"

"Huh?"

"Miff Kreiger!"

"Take that damn thing off!"

"How are ya, Ms. Kreiger!"

"General Hospital's about to start."

"Cool, let's yell at the TV. Her face, right?"

She joins the yelling with a laugh.

*"These damn girls and their long hair.
I just don't get the current style.
Hussies. Yuck."*

◄►

Hallway Snapshot: Hey Bernice

Hey Bernice
Lend me your Cadillac
So I don't have to walk
over this broken glass
They smashed on our road

The other old ladies
Have jalopies with tennis ball wheels
But you, you shuffle in style
The only one in town
Your hearing aids sound like crickets
in your hair when you give me a hug
A grandma's boomin' system

Hey Bernice
Lend me your Cadillac
To lean on

Cities on a Hill

I read your goodbye note
You didn't have the heart to
finish the sentence
But I get it
I'm blessed hospice has Wi-Fi
I can't even type when I'm tired

Hey Bernice
I saw your stuff hastily stacked
Tossed
Trashed
By tough hands uncaring
At the side door
Won't you need it anymore?
Oh....
And the tow truck
Coming for your Cadillac.

Hey Bernice

Lend me a chair.

Josh Urban

Chapter 10 - *Time Passes*

The cicadas chortle the virtues of July, shrilling in the trees above the parking lot. Inside the plate glass windows, it's a quiet, air-conditioned glum.

"Till September?" Coach's eyes bug out. "I've gotta stay in my room till September?"

Raising my eyes from the floor to dare another look, I return his despairing gaze.

"That's what they told me."

Everything is flat. Even my voice. My hands, too heavy to protest, rise halfway, then fall to my sides with a single bounce, compliant.

***

August tests the endurance of the trees. The weak leaves fall, cluttering the sidewalk in a withered brown. Tonda from Activities sweeps them up, disinfects the table in the wedding-style tent, and goes to get Coach.

His son is due in for an outdoor visit. Summer has brought a small concession. People can start to see each other—sort of.

Nate arrives after showing his COVID test results at the front desk, and sits on the far side of the table, per law, no hugging, per law.

Tonda wheels Coach up, then sits in the corner to supervise and enforce, as she's mandated, trying not to listen.

I wave, off to deliver groceries for Ms. Harriet. She used to come to the parties. She used to be able to hear. Now she's stuck, sitting in her wheelchair all day in the doorway of her room.

She can't read lips through masks. She looks confused. I have shopping bags. She can't hear the chalk squeak on the blackboard anymore, but reads the big letters intently.

THESE ARE FROM YOUR SON.

She looks at the groceries. "Oh!"

I point to the window. There he is, cupping his hands to see through the tint, and waves. She waves back. I put the flowers in a vase.

***

September dawns blue and unyielding. No change in the weather. No change in our fortunes, except Coach took a nasty fall. He just doesn't seem himself. Everyone is worried. Not Mr. Coach.

The CDC tells us just a little longer.

Again.

***

Ms. Harriet is declining. I deliver more groceries, and a stupid joke on the chalkboard.

Her head bobs with a weak laugh, silent to both of us.

***

October ambles up, a postman without a letter. Still no change. Except Coach. He's getting bad. It's a Thursday when they let Nate inside for a "compassionate visit."

His daughter and son-in-law arrive a few hours later. We sit at a picnic table by the parking lot, and talk about what to talk about. Sometimes I look down at the boards of the bench, and notice how rough they are, blurred by something in my eye.

A heavy silence. We rise.

"You got this."

Two hours later, Jan's cigarette smoke curls blue in the air as I supervise her afternoon smoke break, mandated. My phone dings with a text from Coach's daughter.

My father died.

"Excuse me, Jan, I've got to go."

The sidewalk bends like a pretzel in the Indian Summer heat, shimmering in finality, surreal.

Paint this, Salvador Dalí. Death twists my horizon ninety degrees.

I walk them out. All is silent except the rustling of their required hospital gowns.

***

Handshakes and hugs are the new Prohibition. The funeral parlor is a speakeasy. The director looks the other way. The carpet seems as deep as a grave, and as silent.

The doorman screens everyone's temperature prior to entry at the service. I'm let inside. Someone fumbles with a laptop for the Zoom stream.

We sit at Cracker Barrel afterwards, and talk about life and loss. His family would make anyone proud. I learn about grace and a meaningful life.

That evening, I run to the stars to escape my grief, or perhaps sit with it. There's a space to visit between feeling and thinking. I'm the only one at the observatory.

A tiny galaxy swims into the telescope's eyepiece, trillions of miles distant. On earth, the mist creeps up from the marsh. I sit back and wonder.

Rest In Peace, Coach.

***

Halloween arrives, and I crank the tunes in the hall. The costumed staff runs from room to room, laughing and clattering. "Trick or treat!" The residents crinkle their eyes, and probably grin behind their masks, handing out provided candy.

After the racket fades, I sweep up the straw.

My scarecrow costume has a design flaw.

I pick up a piece, and look up, smack into the closed door of Coach's old room. I wonder if I'll end up a trail of straw, scattered to the wind, only a button nose and a stray latex glove remaining.

***

Ms. Harriet is dying. The hall is hushed in an afternoon slumber. I sit with her for a spell. Or maybe she sits with me.

The chair next to a deathbed is holy. Her breath rattles. A nurse stops in to check. Then we're alone again. Rattle, silence, rattle. The three pm sunlight is golden. "Goodbye, Ms. Harriet." A bow of the head, a stir of the feet, a dazed walk down the hall. She leaves fifteen minutes later.

The chalkboard sits in the office for weeks. Nobody erases the letters.

THESE ARE FROM YOUR SON.

***

Still no family allowed inside. Cold weather means a propane heater in the outdoor visits tent.

Things become so arbitrary, even top bosses throw their hands up. What will they think of next? People are skilled at normalizing absurdity, though.

Don't forget to wipe down the counter. Someone might have leaned on it.

The portable visit trailer has arrived, awaiting final approval. That enclosed space—a rental construction office in a former life—is deemed safe while a room is not. It sits out front, tombstone gray, with all the charm of Soviet art. The State has a particular style, no matter where or when.

***

Thanksgiving is on a Thursday. That's the only thing normal about it.

It's the First Floor's turn to eat in the dining room. Second and Third will have to wait their designated days.

The linen covered tables are six feet apart.

***

It's beginning to look a
lot like Christmas.

Hallway Snapshot: Rose

I brought her a palm for Sunday once
From the second church
(The first one was guarded about their holy botany)

We watched mass on the livestream
I saw her in hospice when she was dying
(not of COVID)

Surfacing through a morphine sea

She smiled at me.

Josh Urban

Chapter 11 - **Christmas Elves**

November 30th, 2020

Email excerpt from the Executive Director Steve:

"Our resident DJ Josh Urban has volunteered to be our Holiday Elf this year. Here's his message:

"Hello, everyone! Josh, the music man, here with some Christmas cheer.

The restrictions are making it tricky, but, I'm here to be your Christmas Elf. Drop off decorations for your family, and I'll help them deck the halls. Let's make the best of it. Put my name, their name, and room number on the box, and it'll get taken care of. - Josh"

"More boxes for you, Josh."

Charlene gestures to the mail table. The boxes and bags and crates and Charlie Brown Christmas shower curtains and family heirloom ceramic trees arrive steadily.

"No Christmas lights on the trees" Bill the facilities director informs me gruffly. "They're a fire hazard."

I go above his head, and check with Steve. The order stands.

It's a microcosm of the pandemic. The rule makes sense in a way, but at what cost is risk eliminated? Life has many vital little joys, and the altar of Safety is ravenous. The more that's sacrificed, the more that's asked.

I'm cleared for battery powered lights.

The Great Christmas Effort

"Josh, post this Christmas Elf thing on Facebook. Get folks involved."

"Cool idea, Mom."

Soon there's a box of hand drawn cards from a friend's elementary school.

Claire, an old Latin dance buddy, and her husband send a million socks and soaps, plus signed cards and money for gifts.

"Buy the old folks something!" The gifts pour in.

Ms. Calloway's niece emails me for a head count. Her aunt is new there. She'd like to do something. A gift bag for every single resident shows up.

The pile of socks and soaps and cards is growing every day in the activities office. It's already a chaotic place.

There hasn't been a director there since May, and the activities ladies are striving gallantly under text-message assignments from the front office.

They look up from a break. I fumble with some wrapping paper.

"Nine hundred and ninety nine bars of soap in the pile, nine hundred and ninety nine... you take one out, wrap it around...OOO, my finger! Ouch! Stupid paper."

"Need some help, Josh?"

"Yeah...yeah I do, Marie."

A few days pass.

"More boxes for you, Josh."

And...Action!

Santa gets it done. So do these ladies.

Tinny sounds of Christmas carols blare from a tiny speaker. The bingo cart is laden with gifts, and the hallway rings with knocks on doors. Why use a chimney when you've got an access card?

Everyone gets presents. Everyone gets cards. Battery powered lights glow on trees, light in the darkness.

Humans are funny. We're so good at getting stuck, and unstuck, and the only common factor is our own nature.

Christmas is celebrated on Zoom.

An Atonement

"Josh."

"Yeah?" I pause, mid-stride.

"You took all the credit for the Christmas Elves."

Marie's voice shakes slightly. This is new. She's always quiet. Early in the pandemic, it was just the two of us in the Activities department. Everyone had quit in fear or loathing. But not her. She did activities, I did music. There were more of us now, but she had been first. Something is wrong.

"Huh?"

"Yeah – we all worked on this together, and then there's these emails that the bosses are sending out saying Josh did Christmas so well... But what about us?"

"Oh my God, Marie. You're right. I'm so sorry."

I had come up short again. It kept happening.

The lockdown broke some of the old people, and drove them insane. The pandemic, or properly stated, the reaction to the pandemic, put corruption on the daily menu.

It's easy to notice it in other people. It's ghastly to realize the rust on your own heart.

I became the Activities Director a few months later. I always made sure to credit the ladies after Marie's bravery.

It didn't atone, but they forgave me anyway.

A Loss of Innocence

The summons arrives in the hall, casually, offhandedly, a single raindrop.

"Josh, we need you up on the second floor. Mr. Rich doesn't want his COVID test."

Reading history, I never picture myself as the bad guy. I'd always show up in my spaceship time machine ready to stop the mob. (Wouldn't you?)
Now I'm not so sure.

Part of four, I gently hold his left arm down. The ease sears my hand.

I could do this all day.

The scratchy flannel of his shirt erases a cherished idea of myself.

They swab his nose. He yells, not understanding through his dementia.

"You guys are in for it. Next time I see my buddies..."

Everyone leaves. He's fine. I'm not. I kneel on the vinyl floor, sick, talking to him a bit, trying to make one of us feel better.

It doesn't work. Now I know.

It's easy to see the corruption in the head nurse with eyes like cages, breezing past a daughter in tears.

"I can't do in person meetings because of COVID....and I'm done for the day. We'll discuss her mother's transfer to the dementia ward over the phone or email."

Out the door she goes. The daughter's mouth opens, closes, stifles a sob.

But me? Wasn't I supposed to be the "good guy?" What made me think that? Default? Point of view? The lack of bad action? The absence of orders to follow?

Suddenly, there's a ripple on the tranquil lake of my morality. Something dark and terrible has stirred it. Something that's related to the other Somethings that made this whole thing happen. Something that's tisk tisked when visiting the Plantations, the Memorials, the moments of silence, the "othering" of the bad men of history.

It's cathartic to assume that we could never do that. We thank the historical tour guide for showing us our modern virtue, stainless in the present day, a product of the post-sin world.

We're simply too enlightened to be monsters.

Why do we assume the mantle of un-earned sainthood, or at least common decency?

God bless Marie for saying something. God bless Mr. Rich for yelling.

Burkoski mentions bountiful evil in the average person. He's not being theoretical.

Solzhenitsyn talks about how the line dividing good and evil travels through everyone's heart, not a certain group of people. (If it were, it could be exterminated. But it can't be.)

I watch myself now. Closely.

Josh Urban

Hallway Snapshot: Cheesus

Ruby has a way
of calling me over
To her lunch table

So I'm not a staffer
And she's not a fading old lady

Who pays too much for her double room.

But the grandma that she is.

"Saved you a little something."

And slips me an extra mozzarella stick
In a paper napkin

As plain as our days.

As ordinary as

The Eucharist.

Hallway Snapshot: The Rugged Old Cross

_____

There's no polite way to carry
a rugged old cross
In to work

But they're used to me by now.

I made it in my shop
¾ size life, table saw spitting blue smoke and barn board

My heathen mind
Finally realized
There hadn't been church in a year

So we all do something about it
And watch a giant screen in the dining room.

◆▷

Hallway Snapshot: His Majesty's Grace

────────────

Old Louis Fitzpatrick
Sits locked in
A one-bedroom Bastille.

Or so I thought.

Look where assumptions got Robespierre.

"Oh he's alright" A friend tells me in the stale hall.
"Said he's content, feels like royalty. I call him King Louie.
But not the last one."

So that's how it's done.

We doff our caps to His Majesty's Grace.

King Louie
Wears his golden crown around his eyes
Two circles
To better see today's paper
A rustle, and it's on the stack
A year high

Patently—he watches

The birds, through a dirty window
And the news on a TV screen

Etched icy clear from the inside with the anchor's venom.

"My kidneys finally gave out" he tells me, softly.

I groan like Bertha in Room 107, who insists dialysis is hell
Whenever she returns, pincushion purple

To curse existence.

But he's certain of God.

Tuesdays and Thursdays find him talking with the needle girl

Who isn't.

Josh Urban

Hallway Snapshots: Irene

Cat posters, and cat puzzles, and cat pillows
and the real thing got old and died
Poor Ms. Irene.
We all mourned with her.

Months of masks and a crushing quiet
That even hearing aids couldn't fix
No real meows
Just the beeping of the nurses' radios
And the mockery of eye shadow of the anchors
Telling us to be afraid
A hallway bingo set up
on Zoom
so she could join in with
the game around the corner

Then the lady on the third floor checked out
Or went off
Or died
They never really said 'round the halls.
Rules were the official reason.

Cities on a Hill

Tiger was left behind.
Tiger needed a new home.
Irene loved Tiger.

Tiger sat on our card game and accepted a petting.
Irene chuckled, and scolded him, and ruffled his ears,
and had a living thing in her room to care for and
feed and cherish and all the things she used to do when she
was a globetrotter and a young mother
and a woman in love.

Tiger tripped Irene, put her right on the floor,
like a furry mobster
Who promised more next time

I sat with her after they took him away
In silence, letting her go first

"They say I can't have a pet, and I know they're right, so..."
Her hand dropped back to her lap.
We just sat there, pinned by the weight of it all.
Her black eye had a tear in it
And so did mine.
And so did the stuffed rabbit in the corner.

Josh Urban

Chapter 12 - *The Redemption of Miss Golden*

Is Life an endless swell of mediocrity, or does something glimmer beneath the surface? Do people change? Can people change? A tiny lady who lived near the elevator taught me a few things about this once. But first, she had to die.

The Burying Ground

Goodbyes are hard, and as regular as bingo at Statler Place.

But paying respects is a privilege.

There are only a few of us here. She doesn't have any family to carry her. The handle glitters in the weak January sun, waiting for me.

Miss Golden's casket threatens to pull me down with her.

She had been light in life, but the Eternity adds fifty pounds. Grief feels like trying to catch a stone sinking into deep water.

I'm a first time pallbearer.

The January wind creeps out from behind the cedars, raw. It ruffles a few dingy plastic flowers in this cheap corner of the cemetery in the bad part of town. A scratch to my face, and then it heads off to buffet the steam from a nearby factory.

Life goes on, and so does commerce.

The priest's water bottle is generic. This isn't a Deer Park parish. "In the name of the Father..."

He laughs gently, almost playfully, flinging holy water towards us.

Mr. Ronald sits frozen.

Will he blow a gasket as the drops splash his hard Kentucky face? He doesn't seem to notice.

What is rain to a drowning man?

My mind drifts back to a warm September afternoon when I wheeled Miss Golden outside to smoke.

We sat and talked about things little and big.

"Did you ever get married?"

"No" came the reply through a blue cloud of Camels.

"Close?"

A pause.

"Well...Mr. Ronald never asked."

The wind cuts again, bringing me back to the present with a shiver.

There's Mr. Ronald on this bitter January hillside, inseparable since they were twenty, left behind.

He sits, stupefied in his wheelchair,
parked on the tacky astroturf that covers the fresh
clay.

He stares into her grave, as if someone will
push him in next.   Oh, Mr. Ronald.

There's something unbearably heavy
about average sunlight and ordinary days.

The Debut of Miss Golden

One fine summer morning, when the blue
masks would have matched the unseen sky, I met
Miss Golden.

We fell into an honest conversation,
reserved for children and the old.

"Oh, you're from Mississippi?" The question is eager. Delta blues is sacred to me.

She hesitates at my enthusiasm. "Not everyone likes to hear that." She looks like Mick Jagger's sister, but her words are hushed, faded, ashamed. I lean in.

"Why?"

"...The prejudice."

"Are you?"

"I was."

"Are you still?"

"No, but it took me a while...seventy years. I moved to the city when I was twelve. The first time a black man sat next to me on a bus I thought I'd die."

"So what changed?

"I got to know people."

The Days of Miss Golden

"Hi beautiful". Oni's purring Nigerian accent sparks joy in Miss Golden's nearly blind eyes.

The old woman laughs a rueful little laugh, because she wishes she's still beautiful, and knows she's not. The kind nurse reminds her she's a woman, valued and appreciated.

Oni is a savior on the banks of the Styx, answering the call, soothing burning foreheads at three am. Today she's on day shift, holding an ordinary Wednesday together.

"Here's your medicine. How are you feeling?"

"Fair. Thank you, darlin'."

***

"I'm afraid I'm going to die." Miss Golden trembles. My plastic isolation gown rustles. I crouch next to her. She might have COVID (she doesn't).

"Yeah?"

"Yeah."

The silence gathers, fog on my goggles.

Sometimes aspirin is in a little white pill. Sometimes it's in a little white lie.

"I think you'll be OK."

I come back later. She's sleeping. Oni keeps a vigil of friendship in the chair next to her beloved patient. Her dark arm stretches across arctic linen, white as Miss Golden's hair, gloved hand clasping the frail hand.

If only she can hold firmly enough to keep Miss Golden here on Earth.

Oni knows she can't hold the blue veined hand forever, but she can now when needed, so she does.

The image of change, possibility, and love sears into my wondering eye, choking me with a happy tear. The door closes quietly behind me.

The little white lie wasn't, after all. She recovers.

The Death of Miss Golden

Abebi, the nurse, is Oni's work sister, and loves Miss Golden just as much. They call me over with a worried look. Miss Golden can barely sit up in her wheelchair. They've dressed her carefully for the January day.

Oni gives the old woman a pat on the puffy pink coat. It's time to smoke.

I take the handle of her wheelchair, oh so light.

The afternoon cigarette is dear to Miss Golden. I'd often sit and tell her about the stars she couldn't see anymore. She'd tell me not to repeat her mistakes.

"Get married, and have a big family... eight kids!" with a lurch forward, emphasizing the point.

"EIGHT?"

"Yes, eight."

Something is different this time. I bring her out to the porch. She lists to the left, unable to hold up her cigarette. I'm not sure at first. Cigarettes give you cancer. But cancer happens in the future.

There won't be one for Miss Golden. She's been fading each day. I hold the cigarette to her lips for her, a Holy Communion of Tuesday, as if we were both smoking for the last time.

This is time for a deathbed conversation. We both know it, but chose silence as our medium, soaking in a last bit of the precious winter sun.

A breeze twirls the column of smoke, but that's not what makes my eyes smart. I break the silence, describing a robin she can't see, my words measured, numbered, noticeable, count-able grains in the hourglass now.

It's time to go inside. The sacredness of the cracks in the sidewalk dazzle me as I wheel her chair over them, oh so lightly.

Copper trees reach against an ordinary suburban sky, and wave a last goodbye to Miss Golden.

The Rest of Miss Golden

The wind cuts again on its return trip from the factory. There aren't enough mourners to block it out. Only Mr. Ronald's family and the two nurses are here. She has nobody else.

Miss Golden's voice echoes in my head, making sense now. *Have a big family. Eight kids.* There's no accompanying puff of smoke. The wind blows again, too clean.

The preacher chuckles gently, inexplicably, effeminately, as he sprinkles the holy water, his dark hand glistening.

"In the name of the Father, the Son, and the Holy Ghost."

Here we stand in the shadow of the city,
fifty thousand miles from the Mississippi delta,
and light years from a young Miss Golden's freak
out on the bus.

It's Martin Luther King day.

"She's gone to...be with the Lord"
Abebi says, her Nigerian accent thick and
choked, bleeding at the loss of her friend. She
points to the sky, blue like our masks.

I turn, and walk away with Oni and
Abebi. I'm heavy with grief, yet gladdened.

Miss Golden learned to see people
for people. She let in the love of the world.

Here Lies the Redemption of Miss Golden.

Josh Urban

Chapter 13 - *Over My Head*

Leon Wilbur is a tough old fellow, a gnarled piece of barn board with clear eyes. He's gone ninety odd rounds with Life. It beat deep lines into his face, and flattened his nose. But on he goes, breathing audibly, a bulldog of a man, with a walker, then a motorized cart, now a wheelchair.

I like him.

"You're late" he barks from his table.

"I know, I know, I'm sorry." A flustered wave of the arms, then I push the DJ cart over the bump of the lunch room carpet.

Leaning back, he narrows his eyes, watching me set up. He's handsome like granite, worn down from a towering mountain of youth. White hair crowns the cliff of his face. Brown eyes gleam from the crags, sparkling with intelligence—and sadness. His nose drips into his soup.

The PCR tests, forgetting their margin of error, all came back clear. Lady Luck, that unseen feline, has let us mice scamper for a few weeks.

(A positive test result is rarely "symptomatic" at the community, but it doesn't matter. *Back to lockdown. Stay safe.*)

The Mice are allowed to eat in the lunch room, one per table, six feet apart, all facing the same way.

Noontime is supposed to be show-time with DJ Josh.

"I'll do better tomorrow, promise." I push play, and the music starts.

The Geology of a Life

I stop by and visit often during my hall rounds. He tells me stories. The lines in his face start to make sense.

"My father was a real bad guy." Leon looks down at the floor of his tiny room. "Beat my mother, then dropped her off in front of the hospital. I was there.

Helped her to the maternity ward where she gave birth to child number thirteen."

The days blend, making usual markers tacky. *Have a great weekend* sounds harsh, a taunt, a mockery of times when seasons were felt and hugs shared without a second thought. I learn to check myself. I have lots of practice.

The stories keep surfacing, helping to mark the passage of time.

One day he tells me about his kid brothers dying, how the neighbor boy came running, gasping, tragedy hoarse on his lips. The quarry swallowed the two little boys, pulling them under indifferent Colorado waters, and the neighbor couldn't save them. Now Leon was the eldest of eleven. The Great Depression just laughed in his smooth face.

When it was time, he left home. The military brought him north to Alaska.

Wilburs were frontiersmen. Four kids were born there. Once he fixed a general's reel-to-reel tape player. Work took him to the farthest point north. Did the radar installations cook him?

"They'd have the antennas on when I was climbing on them. My head began to feel a little warm sometimes. I bet that's why I got cataracts."

Two wives were both dead and gone. Two of his children joined them. Here he sits, the old adventurer, locked down in an endless quarantine. He tells me he thinks of them.

Sometimes he stares out the window at the birds. Sometimes he looks up at the giant map of Alaska on the wall.   But he doesn't drown his sorrows anymore. He's sober now.

If TVs were magic and little men were behind the glass, looking out as Leon looks in, John Wayne is proud.

The Light of the Ordinary

The halls are numb and repetitive. The days blur, and Fear clamps down hard. How does one manage a time like this? What happens when everything is inverted? Is the World the way it is (or *was*) because of an accident, or because it works?

What happens when all of the nuance — and risk —of Life is sacrificed to one goal?

(And for all the sacrifice, the goal isn't met?)

A phantom haunts everywhere, from the halls of Statler Place, to the aisles of the grocery stores. It's reflected in the glint of TV screens, and shines in the terrified eyes of strangers fighting over toilet paper. Personified, it would be the nerd that everyone kicked and ignored. Now he stands, casting a shadow over the world, straightening his broken glasses.

*I am your God. You will do what I tell you. The Word is with God, and the Word is God, and the Word is **Safety**.*

My shoulders bend under the strain. The First Commandment could be viewed in a new way, outside of Christianity, and religion itself.

Maybe it's a warning of what happens when we choose gods ourselves.

Now we're living the experiment. It's going poorly.

Leon remains real. He keeps me grounded. He comes around when it's allowed, checking out the speakers I use, talking shop.

"Used to work for Philco building radios."

He refuses to be flattened into an "old person" who clueless girls squeal over with a nauseating "Oh, they're so precious."

His bookshelves are stocked with historical accounts and science volumes. I buy him a book on the origin of the electric guitar, and add a field guide to orchids.

"You should have seen them when I was stationed in Thailand" he says often. "They had orchids every color under the sun." What a story to get to repeat. He loans me a book on Masada.

Every few days, usually in the middle of a meeting, my phone rings. "Hey guy...my bird feeders are empty again. Could you fill 'em?" (He's not allowed to leave his room. We're in the middle of another round of lockdowns.)

I swing by, put out the feed, and chat a minute.

"Hey guy, how's the car running?" he asks, keeping that light burning: of real life, of car trouble, grocery bills, and feeding the birds.

"Oh, it's good now. They finally replaced that transmission."

I pick up the faded photo of a pioneer with a rifle. "Who's the guy with the mustache?"

"Oh, a distant great, great uncle. His family moved from the ancestral Wilbur home in West Virginia...do you know, they made the walls two feet thick to fend off Indian attacks? Anyway, yeah, he was a toddler, and they left him in South Dakota. Just walked away. Some locals took him in, and raised him."

The crackled photo gleamed with pride. That man had thrived. A champion. Take that, "mother."

Perhaps the ancestors had helped Leon win the fight with COVID. It had knocked him senseless for a month. I thought he was a goner.

Then one day, the phone lit up my face with his caller ID.

"Hey guy, how ya doin?" the familiar gravel asked. Soon he's back, curious, inquiring, feeding the birds.

Lunchtime Again

"You're late." Leon sits there in the silence, waiting for his soup. He's right. Again.

I kick myself. It's 12:03 pm on a Monday. *Get better, Josh. You keep doing this. Tomorrow's the ticket.*

Tuesday arrives. 11:55 ticked over. I'm early. Leon is earlier.

"You're late." A pause hangs in the air.

"I am *not*. It's 11:55." Flustered again, I point at my watch, then notice his look. Two tables away, the retired school bus driver peers at us intently.

I look back at Leon, then at my watch, then back to him.

"Hey, wait a second."

He leans back with a great wheezing breathy hearty cackle. The mask covers my fish-mouth movements. He's putting me on!

His eyes gleam. He's been teasing me for weeks. I catch up. He's glad.

The school bus driver laughs too, relieved.

The kid finally gets it.

There's The Light of the Ordinary—car trouble, grocery bills, feeding the birds, pulling a joke because we're still breathing. It's still here.

The tiny flame is nurtured, and shines forth.

I join in the mirth. God bless 'em.

Josh Urban

◀▷
Hallway Snapshot: Break 'Em

———————

Rats to dogs
Gain of Function
Long before tony swore it wasn't
The kennel floor turned to
Electric lava
Until the dogs gave up
Ignored the open door
And stood on ten thousand volts
Taking it
Broken

But now
In the present
Realer than a textbook or a moldy telling of barbarism
We're beyond all that

Aren't we?

"Laurie, where is everyone? Don't they want to play bingo?
Lockdown's over for now. It's safe for them to come out."

Cities on a Hill

"They said they'd rather just stay in their rooms."

The plastic bingo ping pong balls rattle in a golden cage.
One escapes, rolling across the floor

That's not lava

But could be

A grinding sound

Loud as the hooves of the White Horse
Echoing in

The Empty Room.

B4.
◀▶

Josh Urban

Hallway Snapshot: Nice Hat

I got him a saw for Christmas
Much to his delight

It's tough being a craftsman away from your shop

It's tougher to lose your second wife.

So we sit here, side by side on the couch
One man bleeding for the Now, the other for the Maybe.

Our plaid is stained invisible red.

"Hey look, we're wearing the same shirt and suspenders, Mr.
Miller.
Maybe I'll look like you when I grow up."

"Hang on a second."

He returns with a matching hat.

Josh Urban

Chapter 14 - *Goodbye My Baby*

The year between Christmas of '20 and '21 is as similar as one handful of sand to the next.

A close examination reveals tiny gems of humanity, loss, heroism, tyranny, and people rising to the occasion.

A long view shows continued lockdowns and the slight concessions of family back in the building for times between positive test returns.

Management's collective panic at family members returning ("All employees must wear appropriate clothes, and please make sure the rooms are clean. Really!") is entertaining.

The joy at the reunions is overwhelming. The frustration at new lockdowns is maddening. A few days on, two weeks off, but progress is made.

By February, it's obvious that I need to move away from the city. The shining potential of any metropolis has been replaced by a menacing glint. It's become a sign of weakness to say "excuse me" in Wal-Mart, and all the stoplights seem to blink obey.

The youthful days of chasing girls at the salsa club and playing outlandish guitar are over. I'm not sure what's next.

Meaning seems a worthy goal, abstract as it is. Still, ships of old could sail rougher seas with a fainter star.

If I think too much about what's been taken from me, I turn my thoughts to the halls where the old folks sit in their doorways.

Then I have to stop thinking before I break something.

A marketable skill is needed. Management accepted my application for activity director, and nursing saved a million diaper boxes for me to pack.

The way that the activities ladies coalesced into a team, and family, will remain a high point of my life. I've also never been so stressed at the other demands of the job.

I change roles back to house entertainer after about six months. Management isn't for me. And it's almost time to move.

The year passes, some die, others soldier on, and voices are still muffled. My house goes to market.

"Good news, Josh! We've got an offer!"

The time comes to say goodbye, voluntarily, with visiting rights.

The Holiday Hush

The little train set's streetlights glow in the dining room. It had been fun decorating it with the crew. Sam even painted a cloud on the background. I look up over my DJ cart at the lunchroom.

People are finally starting to emerge, with floors combining. The tables are still apart, but it feels more like life.

Tomorrow will be my last day. Christmas has come and gone, and most folks will be watching the ball drop on TV. Gatherings aren't in vogue. The moving truck needs to be packed. I try not to think about saying goodbye.

The final song of the set is always "Hello my Baby." Inspired by the *Spaceballs* movie with its dancing alien diner scene, I doff my straw boating hat and wave a show cane. It's become a signature through the lockdown, something absurd and comical.

Hello my baby, hello my darlin', hello my ragtime gaaaaal.

Prancing, stretching out hands, singing to the old ladies in a mask puts me flat on the floor for practical and comedic purposes. I make a bad alien, but the effect works.

Whew!

The Last Day

It's a privilege to say goodbye. I clasp frail hands with paper skin, look their owners in the eye, and try to speak in a clear voice.

"Goodbye. I'll be back soon. I promise."

The day passes in a blur. Wires, some of Leon's old books his daughter bequeathed me, records, office bric a brac, all stack up in the little red car, waiting.

A wave to the chefs in the kitchen, and a thanks for countless grilled cheese sandwiches. A bittersweet laugh with a server buddy as we impersonate each other—our custom. A few more frail hands, a few more promises.

Charlene's nails click on the button. The doors with four paper signs "*Read All Rules Before Entering*" swish open, and then close behind me.

The suburban afternoon is almost normal. Cars roll by, indifferent.

I'm done.

I toss my mask into the trash can thoughtfully. I'd like one last hurrah. But running shirtless through the parking lot seems tacky...

The idea bursts forth like an alien.

The song is cued. The car stereo is UP.

Honk honk!

Three stories of plate glass look out into the parking lot. Behind their reflection, residents sit, looking out. Maybe. It's hard to tell. The afternoon game shows are on.

I honk again, pull my car right in the middle of everything, and leap out. The stereo blasts.

Hello my Baby, hello my darlin, hello my ragtime gaaaal....

The jangle of the piano fills the parking lot.

A dance, a jump, a kick, a bow.

Then a wave.

I get in my car, and drive away.

If there had been a tiny hula dancer on the dashboard, would she have noticed more than the extra gray in my sideburns, and the new lines on my face? Would she have seen the change?

If there had been a tiny hula dancer on the dashboard, she would have misty eyes, too.

* * *

Back at Statler Place, the gray sky is tinted brown through the plate glass window. A few pretzels languish in the bowl on the lonely table.

Martha's gnarled hand reaches for a letter....

Josh Urban

Chapter 15 - *Cities on a Hill*

December 28th, 2021

Thank You - A Salute

It seems like I've been saying "goodbye" for months, but, before I go, I wanted to thank you all for the lessons, and shining examples you've been.

In short, "Thank you for growing me up."

Don't get me wrong, I'll still tap dance badly in the lunchroom when I come back to visit, but thanks for showing me what matters.

For most of my adult life, fun was the goal.

A guitarist by trade, I felt smug that I had "beaten the system" by getting to rock out all day. Still, as time went by, a hollowness crept in, as if the years were corroding the strings.

Recently, the author and psychologist Jordan Peterson made a profound impact with his 12 Rules for Life (my favorite book now). In it he states that happiness is the wrong goal. *Meaning* should be pursued instead, and that is found in the voluntary acceptance of responsibility.

This theory pointed out that I was acting like Peter Pan.

All well and good, but what to do about it? Enter COVID, and you guys. Every day coming to work —mask up, goggles on, the crushing rules, the constant pull to give in to perpetuating the Fear and petty tyranny, the wrestling with uncertainty, and you guys...there you were, walking with calmness, strength, and a steely resolve.

Sure, we all had our days of sadness and desperation, but even quarantined in your rooms, your example shone forth to the rest of us on how to act with fortitude and grace.

"Ye are the light of the world. A city that is set on a hill cannot be hid." (Matthew 5:14, KJV.)

Isn't it astonishing at how true that is? Even locked away, you shone forth. I played over a thousand shows on my DJ cart, and watched.

Every day, picking up that responsibility. Each time, getting blessed with your example, honored to walk together through such an "unprecedented" (how I hate that word) event.

My peers often talk about starting a non-profit to experience meaning. I wish they could have walked with us. I tell them about you often. From the somber task of arriving at the End, to the joyous goofing around and laughs that we shared (and often during the same hour), I will be forever grateful.

You guys are more than adopted grand-parents or friends—we're brothers and sisters in arms. I'm proud to have marched with you.

I'll surely miss the daily path, but I do hope we can stay in touch. You've got my number.

But for now, keep shining.

We all see your good works.

- *Josh*

The End.